PRAISE FOR *THE HUMMINGBIRD*
Winner of the Premio Strega
A *Guardian* and *Spectator* Book of the Year

'Everything that makes the novel worthwhile and engaging is here: warmth, wit, intelligence, love, death, high seriousness, low comedy, philosophy, subtle personal relationships and the complex interior life of human beings'   *Guardian*

'Not since William Boyd's *Any Human Heart* has a novel captured the feast and famine nature of a single life with such invention and tenderness'

Financial Times

'There is a pleasing sense of having grappled with the real stuff of life: loss, grief, love, desire, pain, uncertainty, confusion, joy, despair – all while having fun'   *Sunday Times*

T0343601

'Instantly immersive, playfully inventive, effortlessly wise'   *Observer*

'A tender, beguilingly epic novel ... It's almost only once you emerge from its acutely painful ending that you realise how much of life you have witnessed – the vastness, as well as the richness, of the story'   *New Statesman*

'An inventive, beautiful, complex book'
                                                                  Irish Examiner

'Masterly . . . a cabinet of curiosities and delights, packed with small wonders'   Ian McEwan

'A real masterpiece. A funny, touching, profound book that made me cry like a little girl on the last page'   Leïla Slimani

'Somehow or other Sandro Veronesi pulls off the extraordinary feat of making you believe he is writing for your ears alone . . . a mightily clever novel'

Howard Jacobson

'A remarkable accomplishment, a true gift to the world'

Michael Cunningham

'Ardent, gripping, and inventive to the core'

Jhumpa Lahiri

'Reading *The Hummingbird* is a spellbinding experience; it's so clever, funny and deeply moving'

Roddy Doyle

'I have known for quite some time that Sandro Veronesi was one of the most skilful and profound Italian storytellers of the past thirty years. But *The Hummingbird* is the decisive proof of his sensitivity, of his extraordinary strength as a writer'

Domenico Starnone

Sandro Veronesi was born in Florence in 1959. He is the author of nine novels including *Quiet Chaos* (2005), which was translated into twenty languages and won the Premio Strega, the Prix Fémina and the Prix Méditerranée. His latest novel, *The Hummingbird*, was an instant best-seller in Italy, was voted best book of the year by the *Corriere della Sera* (Italy's most widely read newspaper) and won the Premio Strega. Sandro is only the second author in the Premio Strega's history to win the prize twice.

Also by Sandro Veronesi

The Force of the Past
Quiet Chaos
The Hummingbird

Prophecy

SANDRO VERONESI

Translated by Michael F. Moore

sceptre

First published in Great Britain in 2023 by Sceptre
An imprint of Hodder & Stoughton
An Hachette UK company

1

A CIP catalogue record for this title is available from the British Library

Paperback ISBN 978 1 399 73215 4
ebook ISBN 978 1 399 73216 1

Typeset in Bembo by Hewer Text UK Ltd, Edinburgh
Printed and bound in Great Britain by Clays Ltd, Elcograf S.p.A.

Hodder & Stoughton policy is to use papers that are natural, renewable
and recyclable products and made from wood grown in sustainable
forests. The logging and manufacturing processes are expected to
conform to the environmental regulations of the country of origin.

Hodder & Stoughton Ltd
Carmelite House
50 Victoria Embankment
London EC4Y 0DZ

www.sceptrebooks.co.uk

If he's a hero, then heroes are five-and-dime, and the world is as crowded with them as it is with stray pets, worn tires, and missing keys.

Rick Moody

I know who you are, Alessandro Veronesi, I know your mind, and I say to you that you will do everything in your power to keep your father from dying in a hospital bed rather than, as he wishes, in his own bed, at home, on the first floor of the rationalist building on via Bruno Buozzi 3 in Prato that he designed in 1968 and where you grew up. You will do this for him a few months after you have done the same for your mother. I also know that, consequently, you will assume responsibility for performing and getting him to perform all the home treatments he needs, including the ones to address the frequent emergencies caused by grave comorbidities, and I say to you that you will promise to do this without ever once calling 999, to avoid the risk of hospitalisation, except of course in possible life-or-death situations, which is why I am telling you that, while you are no medical expert, you will take upon yourself the responsibility of distinguishing between such emergencies and possible life-or-death situations – such as an intestinal blockage – and you will do so a few months after having done the same for your mother. I say to you that, despite the inescapable nature of the disease afflicting him, you will try to support your father in mind and in spirit, in such a manner that he never thinks all hope is lost, and every Friday afternoon you will continue to take him to the Pescia hospital oncology clinic for chemotherapy, following the protocols established by Dr Filippo de Braud of Milan and administered there by its chief, Dr Fabio Battaglini. I know and I say to you that you will do this a few months after having done the same for your mother. And when there is nothing more to be done, I know you will dedicate yourself to the proper administration of pain management therapy, following another set of protocols established by other specialists, to make sure that your father does not die in agony. And this, too, you will do after having just done the same for your mother and after having realised what monumental bullshit the whole euthanasia debate is, since the truth you will learn is that *euthanasia is commonly practiced*, at least on the terminally ill, and you will understand this from the casual way that Dr Ciulli, the anaesthesiologist assigned to your mother's pain management, asks you *how deep* you wish the treatments to go, whether to the level he will call A or to the deeper level he will call B, specifying that at both levels the morphine will have the same analgesic properties, and that the difference lies only in the *duration of the agony* – he will say – and as you slowly, but in all likelihood comically, realise what the doctor is really asking, you will be surprised – considering your once cherished convictions – at the scandalised horror you feel, after which, feigning the same casual air by which you might opt for a window rather than an aisle seat, you reply that you would prefer level A, and when, despite your choice, your mother dies in your arms just three days later, and you whisper in her ears 'you're so beautiful', which she won't be able to hear because of the level-A morphine protocol that has heavily sedated her, you will wonder how the fuck much shorter it would have lasted if you had chosen level B – one day? twelve hours? six hours? – and, in short, you will emerge from the experience of your mother's pain management therapy feeling desensitised, if not traumatised, and I know and I say to you that you will make the mistake of telling everything to your father, who will soon find himself in the same situation as your mother, although he will still be lucid and vigilant, and he will immediately demand that when his time comes level B should be chosen without hesitation, and in that moment you won't even realise that your assent to your father's request amounts to a solemn promise, and you will set out light-heartedly on your journey towards the moment when you have to keep that promise, which you will have already forgotten a few days later, since you will be somewhat preoccupied by the thousand and one duties that will start to pile up, also because after the death of his wife the condition of your father will get worse, suddenly and fatally, and you, his son, will be completely absorbed by the ordeal of coping with his deterioration, from the outset, and because I know who you are and I know your spirit, I say to you that you will be overwhelmed by an ordeal that feels much bigger than you, since it will be a question of managing not only the ordinary course of your father's illness – the chemotherapy with all its side effects, the insulin shots for his diabetes and the aggravation of his pancreatitis – but also the extraordinary reality of an organism that has stopped fighting its own decay, and because I know who you are and I know your works, I say to you that you will also take upon yourself the insane task of faking the results of your father's lab tests, and this will come to pass when you notice in his first CT scan after your mother's death that all his tumours have suddenly increased by a shocking one thousand per cent in the past four years, and this will come to pass since you will be the one who goes to the lab to pick up the envelope with the results, so it will be your job to convey them to your father – by phone, since he will be away, on a boat, fishing – and you will realise that you simply cannot tell him the truth, so you will delete a zero from the figures and transform centimetres to millimetres, millimetres to tenths of a millimetre, etc. – and now listen carefully to what I am about to say to you, Alessandro, *you will be shooting yourself in the foot when you do this*, because immediately after you hang up the phone you will race back to the lab to ask the chief who has just signed the report – his name is Dr Lastrucci – to issue a second report that, in a word – you search for the right word – has been *softened* – that's the word you come up with – to accommodate the numbers you have tampered with, and his reply will be an indignant *Absolutely Not*, accompanied by a diatribe against what he will call the contemptible practice of altering lab results *ad usum delphini* – since that's what they call it – and you will have to race to the other end of the city to ask your friend Fabrizzino, the web designer with two Zs, to make a fake report by scanning the laboratory's letterhead as well as Dr Lastrucci's fucking signature, and in the meantime you will call another friend, Paolo, an EMS doctor, to help you find the appropriate words to go with the forged signature, which will have to be chosen very carefully and pondered one by one to make sure they neither reveal the devastating truth to your father nor generate in him any illusion whatsoever of a miraculous cure, after which you will bring the envelope with the forged report to your father, who is just back from what he soon finds out will be the last fishing trip of his life, and you will have to sit next to him while he reads it, fearing that his trained architect's eye will spot the forgery, but he won't, although once he's

finished reading he'll say that these numbers —
despite the subtracted zeros and the carefully
chosen words that accompany them — mean
that he's a dead man, making you regret having
maintained the increase in size of the tumours,
no matter how minimal, and not erasing his
cancer altogether, since now you're talking
bullshit (by the way, Alessandro, since I know
who you are and I know your work, I say that
you will recognise yourself in that awkward
struggle to be sincere while lying), and at that
point, realising that it will never even occur to
your father that you could have forged the
reports, you will get emotional and remember
why your father trusts you, for reasons going
back to a few months earlier, when, confronted
by the catastrophic results of the latest tests to
which your mother had been subjected, and
the consequent idea of asking the chief of the
lab (the self-same Dr Lastrucci) to alter the

results *ad usum delphini*, as you will have learnt to say by now, you were the one to drive the thought from the minds of your father and brother, arguing that a family is united by truth and destroyed by lies, Amen, knowing full well that in reality your mother had absolutely no expectation of reading the lab results herself, and as always would be comforted, so to speak, by the things whispered into her ear by the voices of her loved ones, and you knew full well that it wouldn't be necessary to falsify her results, while at the same time your father will have already been monitoring algebraically the results of his own CT scans and MRIs for four years, using x- and y-axis graphs that he keeps constantly updated so he can follow the curve as the nodules increase, in both absolute value and by single affected organ, boasting that in this way he can predict his life expectancy in real time and with mathematical precision, in other words, my dear Alessandro, I repeat that by falsifying the lab report you will be shooting yourself in the foot, also because, to everyone's surprise, your father will long outlive the verdict that had him for dead – he will outlive it by so long, in fact, that he will require another round of tests (in his opinion), and you will once again have to race to Fabrizzino to falsify the new lab results, and this time you will decide to leave the lesions unchanged, without even a minimal increase, while in reality they have progressed not only to a shocking but really to an unimaginable degree, since the organs under assault by such devastating lesions should have stopped working a while ago and are instead continuing mysteriously to pump, to filter and to secrete, but a little worse with each passing day, which is why I know and I say to you that you will see your father's body deteriorate daily and lose what remains of its autonomy, and you will suddenly find yourself once again having to attend to it, until a sharp pain in the ribs finally makes an appearance, forcing Dr Battaglini to suspend chemotherapy and begin palliative care and at-home pain management, which he will order by quickly typing up on an old Olivetti typewriter – since he never felt the need to equip his office with a computer – the referral form that you, Alessandro, the merciful son, will present to the proper local clinic, again just a few months after having done the same for your mother, a referral application that will be accepted and subsequently forwarded to an anaesthesiologist, who this time will not be Dr Ciulli but Dr Benenato, under whose supervision you will start to administer morphine to your father – first in pill form, 30 mg tablets of MS Contin, one every twelve hours, then every eight, then every six, then 60 mg tablets, then 10 ml single-dose tubes of

Oramorph oral solution, one every eight hours, then every six, then every four – and you'll discover that you have a closer and deeper relationship with his drugged-up body than he himself does, and you'll find yourself manoeuvring, washing and drying, massaging, stimulating and rubbing down his body, and you will become its shepherd, the shepherd of your father's failing body, and you will shave his face with the Braun four-head electric razor you gave him for Christmas, and then, seeing the disappointing results, with a four-blade disposable razor – since they will still not have invented the five-blade model – and you will attempt unsuccessfully to cut his toenails and be amazed to see them repel every attack of the scissors, and finally you will surrender to their yellow impenetrability and call on the services of Giorgia the pedicurist, and you will observe her at work with her professional tools, succeeding where you had failed, restoring to those nails an appearance, a colour and a shape that are somewhat normal, and at one point, on the instructions of his primary care physician, Dr Baroncelli, I know and I say to you, Alessandro Veronesi, you will start to administer enemas to your father, using a Visicol rectal solution, and you will assist him and walk him on his path from the bedroom to the bathroom and set him down on the toilet delicately, and you will slip quickly out of the door and wait discreetly when everything goes smoothly, and when it doesn't – when your father doesn't make it to the toilet in time and empties his bowels into his pyjamas – I know and I say to you that you will console him and clean him with a sponge soaked in Johnson's baby soap, and, confronted by an expression reflected in the bathroom mirror that the adjectives 'humiliated' or 'mortified' fail to describe

– *ashen* is the right word – you will say to him,
*it's no big deal, I've done it a thousand times for my
kids* ... and more bullshit of that sort, and let
me point out that you will do all this for him
without ever having done it for your mother,
since her body will have been lovingly cared
for until the end by her older sister, your Aunt
Anna – she, and not you, will have been her
caregiver – and she will have kept your mother
always fresh and clean and even perfumed, as
you discover when she is in your arms at the
fatal moment, while for your father there will
be no possible care other than what you can
provide, in addition to the episodic assistance of
a succession of home-care nurses on one-week
trial periods who will never win his trust and
thus his intimacy since – remember what I say
to you now, Alessandro – *he who begot you will
never agree to being cared for by a stranger*, and he
will raise every possible objection to anyone,

male or female, whom you bring home for the purpose of taking care of him, and his initial objections will be of a racial nature and will last as long as you bring foreigners, since for tactical reasons he will profess to being a racist, to force you to seek auxiliary personnel of Italian nationality, who are much more difficult to find, and then, once you have found some very expensive Italian home-care nurses, there will be objections to their character – this one talks too much, that one gets too familiar, the other one has a vulgar laugh – and, in short, I know you and I say to you that he will find a way to guarantee the failure of every probationary week you have negotiated with every male or female candidate for the care of his body in your stead, and I declare that not even this will piss you off because you will be fully aware that he is howling with rage at so unexpectedly becoming a widower, since of course he would never agree to have his dying needs attended to by anyone other than her, and he will only accept your care as her surrogate, and after the care of a night nurse named Lina, after you have trained her to speak to him in a manner that is neither too familiar nor too cold, in a voice that is neither too loud nor too soft, not to talk too much about her own shit or to stick her nose into his, and especially not to laugh in a vulgar way or address him as if he were a crazy old coot, and I say to you, Alessandro, so that you may be fully aware of it from this moment forth, that he will not die peacefully, and it will be your job to prevent him from becoming too nasty, which is why you will focus on the administration of morphine sulfate to his pain-ridden body, but from the start I know and I say to you that you will find yourself once again consulting Dr Benenato on the still unsatisfactory results of the protocols he has prescribed, since no matter how high the dose is, your father will still complain about a pain in his ribs not unlike – he will say – a scorpion's sting, a complaint so persistent that Dr Benenato will state that your father's response to the internationally recognised pain management protocols should be considered *abnormal*, and then when he dares to violate these protocols by adding a little benzodiazepine, by which I mean a half-tablet of Halcion, for the sake of experimentation, I know and I say to you that your father will plunge into a deep coma-like sleep, from which he will reawaken thirty-six hours later without remembering anything, hungry and with the usual pain in his ribs, and at that point you will think the excursion outside the protocol is the first step toward the notorious level B – which you will remember only at that moment – and you will mention this to Dr Benenato, asking whether the use of a sleeping pill did not mean that level B had been reached, in a sense, and while saying this you will feel the same shudder of horror as when level B was evoked in your mother's case, and listen carefully now, Alessandro, do you know what Dr Benenato's response to your question will be? The exact words he will use, I know them well, are: *what do you mean by level B?* To which you will respond by repeating confusedly the claims of his colleague Dr Ciulli regarding the two different depths of pain management, and like Ciulli you will call them level A and level B, and like him you will mention the difference between them in terms of the duration of agony, and Dr Benenato will listen in silence and then, smiling, tell you there is no such thing as level B, and seeing the perplexed look on your face he will repeat, staring you in the face, *there is no such thing as level B*, and he will tell you that your shared duty is to alleviate your father's pain and not to decide how long or short his agony should be, and your father will not be in agony at that moment anyway, and he will tell you all this with a pure heart, adding that if so far the two of you have failed, since your father's response to the official protocols is – and he will repeat this – abnormal, this doesn't mean that the two of you will keep failing, and he will immediately start looking for a protocol that will produce the desired response, and he will actually find one that will finally alleviate the pain in your father's ribs, and I know and I say to you that this will produce forty-eight beautiful hours, Alessandro, peaceful hours during which he will pass the time resting or eating or speaking with you or on the phone with your brother or even working on his model boat, a Pen Duick IV, a little out of it, of course, on account of the high dose of morphine sulfate, but without suffering even slightly, and finally you will feel like a good custodian of his body, and finally peace will descend over the two of you, but sadly I know and I have the duty to say to you that once those forty-eight hours have passed, your father's response to the protocol will return to abnormal, since he will suddenly plunge into the darkest paranoia and start to lash out constantly, by day against you – accusing you of being a traitor, a liar, a pimp – and by night against Lina the nurse – the whore, the thief – forcing Benenato to change the new protocol, and quickly, despite the disappearance of physical pain, since the mental pain caused by the paranoia will be infinitely worse, but sadly – now listen carefully to what I am about to say to you – from that point on, and until the end, no matter what protocol is followed, *the paranoia will not go away*, even when the pain reappears, and to make a long story short and arrive at the hour of the truth of this prophecy, for all three of you — Benenato, your father and you, but especially for your father and you — a really awful period will begin, both for your father since he will continue to veer between pain and paranoia, with rare moments of untroubled lucidity, and for you since by persevering in your intent to bring him comfort you will continue to fail and continue to see him suffer, even if in one of those rare, peaceful moments of neither pain nor paranoia you will manage to admire for one last time his blazing intelligence when you come across him at around eleven o'clock in the morning watching a TV show on Channel 4, a show he has never before watched in his life, and you will ask, 'Why are you watching this show that you don't like, Dad? Why not take advantage of this moment to finish the Pen Duick IV model, since you're almost done, or print a few photos of Mom, work a little on the short films of your youth, write or do one of the many other things you like to do?' And his answer will be memorable, Alessandro, prepare yourself to remember it so you can bear witness, since I know and I say to you that he will stare at you with eyes narrowed to slits by disease and he will say to you, 'My son, I watch these shitty programmes to fool myself into thinking that life really is this rotten, that there is no love, or beauty, or intelligence, or challenges, or accomplishments, no nature, sea, wind, or sailboats, but only a lousy mix of grudges, gossip, fear and an airless stench, like these shows would have you believe. So you see, TV makes it easier for me to take my leave,' and he will go back to watching Channel 4, and his words will pierce right through you because you will realise that you never thought about how *useful* it might be, for someone taking his leave of this world, to see such a lousy depiction of life, so in a way these shows do serve the purpose (accidentally, of course, and never occurring to the people – a curse on them, while we're on the subject – who write and produce and direct and market them), as I was saying, of providing an *exit strategy* for the terminally ill that is the perfect way to make their leave-taking less painful and give it a merciful fade-out – but also, Alessandro, now I say to you that his lucidity will last only a few hours and after his afternoon nap he will wake up in the grips of both paranoia and pain, and howling at the top of his lungs he will blame you and order you to take him away, away from there, away, and I am sad to say that unfortunately you will not understand, and you will take him at his word and answer with all the kindness in your heart that you can't take him away, that he's already home, and you will remind him that he always said he didn't want to be left, etc., and he will grow exasperated and almost weep and despair and shout and argue that you promised him, and you still won't understand, and you will stop contradicting him to avoid pissing him off even more, but you will continue to take him at his word and you still won't understand what he's asking you, but you will do it anyway, you will telephone Benenato and tell him there's an emergency, and Benenato will be in the vicinity and he will come in person in the space of a few minutes, and your father will thank him and immediately calm down, and he will calm down even more when Benenato decides to inject him with morphine, using an intramuscular syringe, and when he leaves, he will tell you that if your father doesn't calm down and doesn't fall asleep after the injection, he'll toss out all his textbooks, and your father will thank you and ask you to lie down next to him, and he will take you by the hand and make you promise to scatter his ashes – which for some reason he calls *sands* at that moment – in the sea at the same spot where, a few months earlier, you had scattered the ashes of your mother, and you will understand suddenly – finally – you will understand what he meant when he pleaded with you desperately to take him away, and a profound and solemn silence will fall over the two of you, during which he will bless you silently, while you, Alessandro, dumbfounded, will be shocked that you didn't understand, that you didn't remember, and you will realise that all your father wanted for his body, when you were knocking yourself out trying to look after him, was death, and that all he expected from you, from the moment he had begun to express himself in such a, let's say, symbolic way, was for you to administer the level-B protocol that you had mentioned to him, *and that you promised to administer to him*, and, in short, you will find yourself observing your father at what he thinks is the last moment of his life, grateful to you, his son, for having finally procured it, and while he is absorbed unfathomably in who knows what unfathomable thoughts, which he thinks are his last, I am sorry to have to announce that your own thoughts will be really stupid, even obscene, because when you see him arranging himself on the bed next to you to find the perfect position in which to die, his eyes closed and his hand in yours, you will think of Oliver Hardy, yes, of that sketch when he thinks he's been hit by gunfire but wasn't really, and he sinks down very slowly, moaning, and lies on the floor, more and more slowly, moaning, looking for the right position to die, and this will be the thought that comes to you when you are with your father during what he thinks is his final

hour, in silence, a silence he will break, at a
certain point, by saying, 'Well? Get on with it!'
– obviously ready to start protesting at that
point, too, already on the verge of getting into
an argument over how long it's taking for what
he thinks is the fatal overdose of morphine
sulfate to kick in – and then you will reassure
him, you will tell him that the injection takes
effect very slowly, and you will assure him that
soon he will nod off, even if you're not at all
sure that he will, especially after Benenato's
remarks about tossing out his textbooks, and
even if your father obeys you meekly, and
relaxes, continuing to thank you, and gives
himself over to a kind of deep meditation, you
will continue to be fearful and to be worried,
and you will remain tense and anguished until,
I know you and I say to you, you will be literally
overwhelmed by his peacefulness and you will
stop worrying, you will stop being fearful and

troubled, but there will be a new surprise, because when your father seems to be finally *gone*, gone away, forever, his drowsy voice will once again break the silence, and from his death-bed, with his eyes closed and his right hand clasped between your hands, he will start to tell you about the time he met Frank Lloyd Wright, the year before he died, in Milan, when a local entrepreneur, a friend, had invited the famous architect to a meeting to offer him a commission, paying for a private plane from Paris, and your father will describe to you Wright's mythic appearance at the airport, his white scarf, the long overcoat, the 'low-brimmed cap', as he will call it, that you will know is called a Pork Pie, made famous by Gene Hackman in *The French Connection*, after which you will barely register that his story has already jumped to the moment when the Milanese entrepreneur asked Wright to design his new factory, and

Wright replied with a request for an honorarium of one hundred million dollars, which in those days was an outrageous, unbelievable, impossible figure, more than what it would have cost to build the whole factory, making the blood drain from the face of the entrepreneur – who had just stated that cost was no object – and prompting him to formulate an objection, unceremoniously cut off by Wright, who explained impatiently, as if it were the hundredth thousandth time, that once he had designed the man's damned factory, the factory itself, the products that came out of it, the place where it was built and he himself, the owner, would become not famous but *immortal* (like Johnson Wax, thanks to its offices in Racine, or all of Oak Park, thanks to the twenty-three Prairie houses – including Wright's own home – and the Unity Temple, like Mr Edgar J. Kaufmann, the Pittsburgh merchant, thanks to the house over the waterfall, like Harold C. Price, the Bartlesville oilman, thanks to the tower bearing his name), and immortality was the best publicity, so all Wright was asking was to get paid for it, and at this point your father, already half gone, will start to chuckle, and you won't even be able to imagine what he makes of the whims of all the industrialists he's had to please during his career, sacrificing his own architectural rigor without ever being able to dream of taking the kind of revenge that he had seen his idol exact on his Milanese friend – and that, Alessandro, will be the chuckle with which he thinks he is nodding off, so to speak, and by which he will take his leave, and it will still be on his face when you leave the room, already dreading the moment the next day when he wakes back up, already anguished by the prospect of having to submit to the angry outbursts of your deceived father, but at least he will sleep deeply – this time thanks to Dr Benenato's library of medical reference works – while you won't be able to sleep a wink all night long, worrying about the explanation you're going to come up with the next morning for his non-death, and when the morning comes, you will be armed with a first draft of an explanation to be elaborated right there on the spot, off the cuff, depending on the nature and entity of his reproaches, and you go to his house and enter his room and find him busy consuming a large breakfast and ordering liver and onions for lunch, looking energetic, fresh, rested, lucid and completely oblivious to last night's big scene, which – I know you, Alessandro, I know how you think – will immediately make you cherish the previous night, since at that point, free of the quarrelsome ending you were so worried about, it will in fact be the moment of your father's true death, the one he wanted and chose, and you will be the only person in the world to have witnessed it, and I am saying to you, in short, that the anguish that deprived you of sleep will turn out to have been in vain, since your father will not remember having died holding your hand, nor having been grateful to you, nor having told you about Frank Lloyd Wright, and upon reawakening he will be peppy and for a few hours he will even be affectionate, but after that short reprieve he will go back to complaining about a sharp pain in his ribs, and everything will start all over again, with renewed paranoia and suffering and angry outbursts, and you won't be able to help but wonder why your mother's death — so sudden, so atrocious, so treacherous — was accepted by her so meekly and simply while your father's — so expected, announced, prepared for and now desired for by he himself — should be so furiously rejected, and in the midst of these thoughts the telephone will ring and it will be Lina the night nurse who will quit, leaving you high and dry, because of an urgent need to care for her thalassaemic daughter, sparking a new round of arguments about night-time assistance, of ethnic refusals and an urgent search for an Italian male or female nurse who cannot be found this time, however, I know and I say to you that your brother will take charge of the situation and you will receive a visit at home from a quiet, surprising and very young Russian male nurse named Vadim, whom your father will accept without a word as if he had always known it was his destiny, and Vadim will be accommodated in what used to be your grandfather's bedroom, where he will sleep by day so as to assist your father by night, even if there won't be enough time to know whether he is really as good as your brother claims since your father will suddenly take a turn for the worse, and everything will accelerate, and Benenato will increase the dose of morphine sulfate until a kind of drug-induced coma will be reached that is actually not much different from what you had understood when Ciulli first mentioned the level B that according to Benenato doesn't exist, and then you will realise that anaesthesiologists have many different ways of defining the same thing, and the main thing you will realise is that this is the end, and that all Benenato is doing is seconding you, although your father will manage to fool him yet one more time when, thoroughly sedated – according to the protocols – he will reawaken, I mean it, and become sentient enough to say goodbye to your brother, who had been told to return from Rome urgently, and to recognise your brother, smile at him and also ask him to take his hand and to take his leave of him, whispering into his ear something you will not hear, Alessandro, and you will never know, and it will be *their* secret, the same way that the story of Frank Lloyd Wright will belong to you, thereby confirming unto death – this has to be said – his legendary impartiality, his strenuous, scientific striving to make no distinctions between his sons, epitomised by the unforgettable moment when he shouted, 'My son—I take it back. My sons are a couple of assholes!', during a fight with you on a boat sailing in the Gulf of Lipari, a diatribe your brother is completely unaware of, an impartial-ity essential – which the two of you will never truly understand – to his making sure you two brothers would grow up to be two balanced men, and having completed this gesture your father will take leave of his sons and of this world forever, succumbing to the cavernous and irreversible sleep predicted by Benenato's protocol, and at that point it will be a question of hours, of just a few hours, since I know your father will continue to sleep like a sedated lion deep into the night, when you will be asleep in your bed, your brother in his, and Vadim, according to his own version, will have gone to the kitchen for five minutes to have a cup of coffee, and in a solemn, solitary instant your father will stop breathing, and you will be awoken by a phone call from your brother and it will be half past three in the morning, and you will get dressed and go to your father's home and find him dead, and Vadim will be weeping, literally sobbing, and he will want to leave immediately, irrationally, even if you tell him there are no trains at that hour, even though he risks not being paid for the few days of work because neither you nor your brother have any cash, and in short, Vadim will have a nervous breakdown, and, since I know who you are and

I know your mind, you will race to withdraw cash and pay him and allow him to escape into the night, and while you are standing there withdrawing the bills from the ATM slot you will feel alone and tired and abandoned and orphaned, and the dawn will still be far away, and you will lift your eyes to the sky, and the sky will be as black as sackcloth and ashes.